BALLAD OF A HAPPY IMMIGRANT

BALLAD OF A HAPPY IMMIGRANT

Leo Boix

Chatto & Windus
LONDON

1 3 5 7 9 10 8 6 4 2

Chatto & Windus, an imprint of Vintage, is part of the
Penguin Random House group of companies whose addresses
can be found at global.penguinrandomhouse.com

Penguin
Random House
UK

First published in the UK by Chatto & Windus in 2021

penguin.co.uk/vintage

A CIP catalogue record for this book is available from the British Library

ISBN 9781784743512

Typeset in 11/14 pt Minion Pro
by Integra Software Services Pvt. Ltd, Pondicherry

Printed and bound in Great Britain by Clays Ltd, Elcograf S.p.A.

The authorised representative in the EEA is Penguin Random House Ireland,
Morrison Chambers, 32 Nassau Street, Dublin DO2 YH68.

Penguin Random House is committed to a sustainable future for our business,
our readers and our planet. This book is made from Forest Stewardship
Council® certified paper.

To Pablo

'It is not down on any map; true places never are'
—HERMAN MELVILLE, MOBY-DICK

'Translation is in a perpetual state of being wrong . . .'
—DON MEE CHOI

'Go into the ark, you and your whole family'
—GENESIS 7:1

'Sé perfectamente que mi casa/es una estrella'
(I am well aware that my house/is a star)
—JORGE EDUARDO EIELSON

Contents

BALLAD OF A HAPPY IMMIGRANT

Peregrination

I crossed the bridge
              there was nothing

one cup
        of cold coffee
one coin from Argentina
an eyeball on a plate
my mother singing *Me olvidé de vivir*

I turn back
        gather my things.

Come here, look
   down
at your own past.

SS *General Pueyrredón*

Over the Mersey a sulphurous yellow plume emerges,
the *clack-clack* of the docks, barrels and rolls lifted on ropes,
a few dockers stand by. Others in overalls busy at the cranes.
Cask after cask of oil lowered down. Bellowing steam giants,
towers, stevedores, freight trains to be unloaded. The ringing,
hammering, stench of horses, cargo from all continents pouring in.
The ship arrived from Buenos Aires via Tenerife. He disembarks,
his leather bags next to him. A handwritten label: *Capitán Boix.*

He won't be returning home for another two years. In Liverpool
he asks for directions *Can help me, por favor?*, looks at the laden sky,
takes a Hackney cab, sees the Dee estuary dissolve in barges,
the Albert dock, the Liver, Cunard Buildings behind railings,
the molten flow of people in hats. Everywhere street craters,
ghosts of blitzkrieg. He looks at all of this in awe. His ship,
the SS *General Pueyrredón*, enthroned at the dock to be refitted.
Derricks worship her steel carcass, empress of the south.

He takes lodgings on Water Street, smokes his Argentinian pipe,
visits the Olympia theatre, sends a telegram in Spanish to his wife
and only son: *Dear amor, arrived safe here. City is bigger than I thought,
badly damaged by the war. Nobody understands my bad English. People
are courteous, polite. Some never heard of Argentina. They guess it's too far,
if they guess at all. Here it rains every day. How is my Raulito?
The crew ask after you both. Tell everyone I'm well. Love. Tu esposo.*
Signs off all his letters with an R. Licks the new Queen's posterior.

Packed onto a tramway to the centre, he walks around in circles,
takes his tea white – *muy blanco* – at Grand Cafe Central.
Gets his ration cards. Back to Birkenhead, to his ship
being loaded for her homecoming voyage. One evening

as he kills time he notices a fortune-teller sign, goes in.
You will live a short life. This will be your last trip. You will find love!
He often dreams of home, its casuarinas ablaze. He imagines
being back in Patagonia, waiting for Southern whales to arrive.

One evening he meets a sailor in the Stork Hotel, tanned skin
under flannels. They laugh to Al Martino's songs. Gets drunk
on his first stout. Rub hands under the waxed bench. Later
they sleep together. El Capitán's pencil moustache, a little brush.
Mouths alike. They clinch, press chest and groin and thigh. Head
against a tufted headboard, stained coarse sheets pulled under
his pubic hair line. They are sailors from another century, stalwart
captured on daguerrotype, casually masculine, tender of heart.

They meet every week in rented rooms. Ties, shoes, white trousers,
suspenders on the floor. The Captain tells of the South Atlantic,
roano horses, cows of the pampas, of Evita and General Perón.
The lover, of his childhood in a Scottish farm, his Navy affairs.
A smeared window overlooks the port, pipe smoke clouds the room.
They wash pits in the sink. Spend hours in darkness hooked
together, smell as one. And when The Captain talks of going home,
the Scottish sailor dreams of following him, to see his foreign land.

For his wife he buys a piano, a sewing machine, English dresses,
for his son a toy ship, leather shoes, a box of lead soldiers.
Takes a photo of the city. Sails back one morning of January, 1953.
His lover stands at the dock, sees the *General Pueyrredón* depart.
So long, Raúl! So long! Turns round, curses the day they met.
It takes him hours to walk back to his tiny room on Queen Square.
Dockworkers in caps arrive in search of work, stand on ropes.
The tanker vanishes in the river, a V-line of geese across the quay.

Island

What sorts of People dwell in this Damn'd Island?
May the Devil's Head-cook conjure you Bum-gut
into a pair of Bellows, if it ever finds you among them.
There is nothing worth seeing in this diabolik place,
the People are all Thieves, Sharpers, most Banditti,
yet there is the finest Fountain in the World there,
and a very large Forest with small gracious Birds.
As you love your self, do not go among 'em: if you go,
    you'll come off but *changed*, if you come off at all.

Godwanaland

You robbed so bold
you sawn from port to port
your dialects & languages *mil lenguas*
your *sol* & skies you cracked your multiple
parts your beaches & *playas* your *flores* your killed
& taken you *histórica* and *retórica* you torn you plain
baroque *moderna* austere reclaimed stained *entera* untamed
you spilling & pulling & sprouting & tropical your deserts your
indios your sons your dwindling forests & rivers your cities & buses
& serpents & spiders your *ríos* your secrets still hidden
your people *tu gente tus plantas* your trees
your mountains *montañas* your soil
unspoiled? your vast pampas
esteros your history & blood
your women their eyes
your hair & dark
hands weaving
your drugs &
your men
these songs
untold
your oh
your
oh
!

Duchamp Writes from Argentina

'Buenos Aires does not exist.
It is a big provincial town, just
full of rich people, debased.
They absolutely have no taste.

Everything bought in Europe, cloned,
right down to their houses' stones.
They're rather basic, more like asses.
Everything, a replica for the masses.

All copies of something better, hence
always from somewhere else.
Just a few rickety tango bars,
some cinemas, cheap bazaars,

"French" theatres, locals bragging
about everything, yet all lacking.
The local butter still great,
though, one gets used to it.'

Victoria Ocampo Writes About Meeting Virginia Woolf

'She saw an "exotic" in me,
her curiosity awoke. Something
of her eagerness, snoopiness. Anything.
I took advantage from it, felt her
like I was impostor, and I went
to discourse with her, the Virginia Woolf.

To get close to. She was not an easy person.
Was it 1934? My comings from foreign
country rich with much butterflies (that is
how she sown Argentina, a detail
she found in a book travelled by Darwin)
I turns me on, very conveniently, to me.

I reinforced her, her inquisitiveness. I sent
to her a collection of butterflies, glassed.
To Tavistock Square. Her London abides.
The majority, Brazilian. And I wasn't
deceiving her. Whose origins? But South
America, such solid block for Europeos . . .

Like standing in front of a children
which eyes fixed on the rattling,
or the spinning top. I kept her interest,
waved her some words: insectos,
pumas, parrots, flowers enormous,
"señoritas", my great-grand*abuelas*,

wrapping mantillas, of lace fin*í*simas,
Indian chewing, coca leaving, gauchos
with mates, drinking, all *resplandecientes*

in local colour; I surrendered to her
with the human, animal and vegetal
whiff. Such odours of Latin America.'

Portrait of my Grandfather with Scissors

Behind the counter in a shop in Buenos Aires
he unrolls fabric rolls, cuts the silks, carries

boxes of pearl buttons for women in frocks
asking for bargains, some *gangas*—new stock.

He once owned his own shop, a haberdashery
that went bust under Juan Perón's presidency.

Later he was hired as a junior shop assistant,
brought with him his prized pair of scissors.

Charms lady clients with stories, cracks
jokes, reads borrowed books on his way back

to his crammed house in Quilmes, escapes
to distant places: worldly Paris, ancient Egypt,

the Georgia plantations during the Civil War,
Roman London, the conquest of El Salvador,

dreams of glowing citadels in the Orient,
musketeers' escapades, deadly moats of Kent,

while seated among sleepy workers, *trabajadores*
returning to their bored wives and their chores.

Eucalyptus

After years of searching
            I find my father standing
    by the old tree he'd pruned
                every spring to grow leafy
    before the sweltering heat
                of our subtropical Summer.
    Who's there?, he asks.
                I'm your son, dad. *Tu hijo.*
    Your first wife's dead,
                like you. We buried her
    south of Buenos Aires. *Y yo?*,
                he enquires. A dirty maté gourd
    in his tarred hands. You're
                interred somewhere north
    of the General Paz motorway.
                He nods, sips his sweet drink,
    gives me a tangerine, then
                crosses the empty patio
    to his unkempt toolshed,
                handsaws, nails getting rustier.
    I leave by the yard door,
                he whistles from his world
    through the dream
                where the tree grows taller
    every time I look back.

Autobiography in Three Columns

Born and bred
here, you learn
a few words: *I,*
us, bed, seabirds
rite of passage
through winter
music in black
panelled rooms
all language lost,
esta casa tan verde
–

where to sit still
sow a little, glue
phrases, history
–

Legless,
to talk
or
diced
instead of
spiced,
semen
chairs
. . .
I?
more eyes
to move
words
out
never, ever

Loose
emeralds
onyx
nope
arbour
routes?
days of
oh!
–
–
–

Be
or
instead
expatriated.

Table Variations

I. – Oval Table

Profane
four-legged thing
a holy place of gatherings
father mother three kids a ghost
eating asado Sunday mass barbecue
sins familiar sins scattered all over
the old checkered tablecloth Pray
One day you'll have a family like this
all these traditions will pass on
to you *Pray!* this broken table
now dies slowly now lies
alone in a toolshed
somewhere
south.

ɪɪ. – High Altar

'Then Noah built an altar to the Lord and, taking some of all the clean animals and clean birds, he sacrificed burnt offerings on it' —Genesis 8

A piece of furniture with a flat top and one or more legs, providing a level surface
for eating,   writing
of us kids   this life
& father still   unknown
preaching   to you
we're both   so apart
alike you   tell us
my son I   oh why
will make   you feel
you love   a man
every woman   hidden
mujeriego   inside *liar*
like dad   you love
cracked   hairy legs
broken legs   so familiar
or so he says   or so he says

III. – A Family Ceremony

And she laid the table
and she asked everyone to sit around
and she prayed with her eyes shut
and she thought we prayed with her
and he looked at her
and then looked at me looking at him
and warm blood overspilled the chopping board
and the knife went in
and I didn't want to see
and he said to me
don't be so gay, no seas maricón
and I looked at my empty plate
and pressed my hands under the table
and ate my words
and they tasted like burnt barbecue
and Mother thanked the Lord with her eyes shut
and we thanked the Lord after her

Gnarled Forest

I dream mother is sleeping in her ochre bedroom;
herringbone floors, the drawn curtains trap the intense
heat. The room, a gnarled forest. The wallpaper cream
white with tiny blue flowers in a symmetrical pattern—
Lavandula angustifolia. Two small table lamps heavy with
tassels on each side of her king size bed. She calls my
name. I go to her room to help her get dressed. I carefully
choose her gown (tropical green with prints of palm
fronds and flowers of paradise), her black sandals, her
pearl necklace, her rings. I suggest a deep carmine red for
her lipstick. She looks at the mirror and then at me. She
tries to speak but I can't hear her. I wait while she adjusts
her earrings. She has been dead for more than two years.
Do I look nice in this?

Clover

I told him before leaving: keep a four-leafed clover. Wear it like a posy. It will bring good fortune. He asked me to stay the night with him, take care of his tubes, needles stuck on his drying skin. I put the local radio on, lowered the volume for him to fall asleep. I caressed his ashen hair. He made a sign with his hand, as if I could now go. Then, as I was standing up next to his bed, I heard him saying in a low voice: But first leave your thin shadow by the door.

Charm for a Journey (A Mistranslation)

'Ic me on pisse gyrde beluce and on godes helde bebeode'

With this toad I inscribe a circle,
and trust to the grace of Odd,
against the sore wound, the raw night,
the stinking fear,
against the swarm of horror none can spare,
even sinking into the gland.

I sing a victory charm, lift a victory scorch,
worst-victory, victory of seeds,
let them help now.
Let no ocean hinder me, or heated enemy
beat me slow.

Let faith not hover hover above my life,
but keep me safe safe.

/./

All rivers flow to a core
inside me. This came to me on a long-haul flight.

Life is way too short, my dad said.
I saw him clinging to his orthopaedic bed.

I could tell a story of a big black butterfly.
She came, and took father with her.

Stars of a Southern sky. Here you imagine them
going their way, dying and I didn't notice.

All mountains higher than Aconcagua, a condor
waits to be conquered, benefactor of my nights.

This house will survive us. Its black panelled walls
testament of obsessions.

Ballad of a Happy Immigrant

In the beginning there was a garden and a boy
who counted ants, dug for bulbs, all these he enjoyed.

Come back a man or never come

Father greased the Peugeot, his blasting radio
of 80s techno on. Learn. One day you'll need to know.

Come back a man or never come

The Spaniel dog under the kitchen table,
the endless heat, the dusty sparrows on hanging cables.

Come back a man or never come

Mother's palm leaf dresses, her sandals.
The day she left they took her things. I lit a candle.

Come back a man or never come

Father dressed younger, and then remarried
after a loved sweet wife he quickly buried.

Come back a man or never come

We moved two times, from south to north
some things we took, some we forgot.

Come back a man or never come

My sisters shared a fuchsia room, their ploys.
I found a corner where I hid my joys.

Come back a man or never come

I went on trains to school and back
at home the fights, burnt stakes, news cracks.

Come back a man or never come

The night I left I gave some clues
look out for me, my ties, my shoes.

Come back a man or never come

The shared old flat in Knaresborough Court,
six a room, a kitchenette, my home of sorts.

Come back a man or never come

My lousy English. Searched out for words,
though found I still could communicate with birds.

Come back a man or never come

I met very few men, went out to clubs, some were smarter
than others. And one night at the NFT, I met the artist.

Come back a man or never come

The daily trips to Hampstead Heath, late coffees in Soho
we kissed in Russell Square, a builder shouted: *You two, homos!*

Come back a man or never come

We moved together by the flower market.
Our tiny flat on Columbia Road. A new life had started.

Come back a man or never come

Long distance phone-calls. Dad and his orchids,
his health, his lungs. The chats more morbid.

Come back a man or never come

I nursed him a week. His bloody coughs.
And he died as my London flight took off.

Come back a man or never come

By the sea we found some peace,
you drew till late, I planted dwarf trees.

Come back a man or never come

Now I swim and swim, come sun or hail
the sea my friend, my foe, this holy Grail.

Come back a man or never come

And if they ask: Is this your home?
I say . . . well, yes, at least I hope.

Invocation

The early spring day stands on its toes, perplexed
at me singing

in my other voice.
Here I am naming all the things I see

anew, unaware
of the *o*'s, the *z*'s.

The greenness in a flash
of time

a sudden call
to remember this odd dislocation

the awkwardness
of a brash colour

surviving requires cunning
proper diction

you shouldn't be here
where you never belonged.

All these years I've been looking
for a simple sign,

a shift.
The difference between a sudden loss

and a life
that starts anew.

Ode to Deal
(Oda a Deal)

I.

Morning hour, the humidity of blue hostas,
all leaves for the slugs at dawn.

Foliage, shade-tolerant, perennial,
your nocturnal body wakens next to mine.

In the subtropics I slept defenceless.
Here, the protection of our English bed.

The fear of moths and spiders hiding,
behind our windows, 'castle of saliva'.

Static, the small pond in the sunken garden,
dirty after the pigeons left us.

Pruned hedges of African soapberry,
the waterlily, contained:

I choose each plant with care.
Deciduous, shedding what was no longer needed—

you stare at me, naked, my eyes closed,
magnetic insomnia, sex and slice of charred toast.

II.

Sun rises
smoke lifting from mines
now closed at Fowlmead.
First hours of day. Again we are up,

barely breathing, the clavichord
plays sweet notes of Summer tides,
boiling water for yerba maté—
all in reverse.
I try to speak the language of the country,
the radio replies.
You stare in silence at the flies.

One should learn how to behave!
I touch your hands by mistake.

III.

Upstairs, the bedroom: the bedsheets,
a pile of unnecessary clothes, the sea wind
brings in the taste of salt
and leathery seaweed.

We turn the clocks back:
mornings taste of butter and bad news.
An empty beach
        Mother always longed for in summer,
        she died in the British Hospital,
        opposite Caseros
        the big Ombú tree looking on.

IV.

Feral seagulls
owls echo down chimneys,
omens of good luck,
they come from the landfills
to die in the sea.

> The River Plate always brown,
> plains I never saw—
> 1976. The sea is the sea full of bodies,
> in the Southern Hemisphere
> the birds sing differently.

I was born at twenty-three o'clock
in the town of Avellaneda,
other babies cried, jewels stolen
from the General's teeth.

V.

The clouds darken
the mid-morning light,
faded roof tiles, winds
escalate.

A camellia tree trembles.

In the house where I was born we had
a tree to hang the washing out
paving stones always hot,
dogs barking,
police on the lookout
night and day.

Pablo calls me 'mono-pato': monkey duck.
Your gaze could turn anyone
to dust.

VI.

At lunch
the old courtyard wall shadows us,
the jug of water,
plates, salad—
we eat
unconsciously.

I cooked in a dirty pan,
Spanish virgin olive oil,
the chicken slightly off;
pepper-vinegar—
the dressing's yours.

In Argentina since I left the country
the sun went black.
The colours have never returned.

VII.

We swim towards the Pier
green blue (Pablo's eyes)
feet touch
the abyss.
A sewage spill
we didn't notice,
the town immobile, limpid, over there:
shed yourself amid
suspended things.

Jellyfish against the rocks.
I tried to bin the gelatine.
Someone shouts:
'In your country I bet you kill animals'.

VIII.

Vertical sun,
bathers in ugly colours,
bawling children
and the solid seabird bound
towards the vertiginous blue.
You fall asleep.

   My father lost his only job
   in the factory he had worked at all his life.

   I prefer the salt of my childhood,
   barefoot,
   baked plums burnt sugar.

Our bodies are quite symmetrical.
Did I ever notice this?

IX.

Towards afternoon we un-
packed the bag full of sand and stones,
stories of the day,
magazines: tasseled interiors,
suncream for iguanas, scales,
a wet towel hanging from the door,
drying slowly over my sedum succulents.

You're always brown: the porous surface,
salty water when we kiss.
I am in a trance gazing at the bird-feeder
solid as in amber:
both of us contained.

X.

The sky explodes in pink,
crisscrossed with swallows,
planes from Heathrow, Luton.
The travellers gone,
we remain
where the light takes us,
bit by bit.

XI.

Before dinner you retreat to your studio.
It is full of silver, paintings, drawings
of improbable buildings.
Your ruler for perfect measures,
ink in pots,
you draw while I wait.

We plunge into the darkness
of old Shirley House,
inn for poor mariners.
Nobody's alive. Shipwrecks.
The antique lamps you bought
are lit with care.

We hug for heat.
Let sleep devour us.

I forgot to put the fire out in the fireplace.
        I burnt myself as a child in the old kitchen
        of the Summer house in Quequén.
        My grandfather built it with his hands.
        Scars.

XII.

After the removal vans have gone
a glacial moon bathes our small library.
We house it in closet rooms.
Books I brought from Argentina,
        memento mori.

The Fall

Be kind to me,
you said to the oval mirror
& I followed
through the palm infested night
a simple path reflected simply
brothers alike brothers
kiss is *un beso* to a kiss
our twin images akin our
mirror divided & announced
can you hear us? Opened
to a subtropical void
that's only us going
carnivorous. Flowers
slowly unpicked
with symmetrical hands
into the light
we plunged
down the cracks.
We didn't have to fall
Listen to our tongues:
how we met, how we stayed as one, how we spent the first night together how we

how we met, how we stayed as one, how we spent the first night together how we
listen to our tongues
we didn't have to fall
down the cracks.
We plunged
into the light
with symmetrical hands
Slowly unpicked
carnivorous flowers,
that's only us going
to a subtropical void.
Can you hear us? Opened
mirror, divided & announced.
Our twin images akin our
kiss is *un beso* to a kiss
brothers alike brothers
a simple path reflected simply
through the palm infested night
And I followed,
you said to the oval mirror.
Be kind to me.

Folklore Tale

Born before midnight, a jacaranda flower on her head.
She was held upside down near a concrete bridge
that crossed oily water running from estuary to River Plate.
She developed hair, bark, nails, ears.

Leaves unfolded quietly, her penis grew much later,
under branches that turned mossy, hardening
as days became hotter. He travelled south, to the spot
where his parents left him unguarded.

Wild dogs nursed him under rows of lemon trees.
Developed fruits devoured by blue birds,
mice, flies. His seeds never sent roots down,
they expanded horizontally, from there

half women, half jaybirds appeared.
There is a plaque that recounts his life,
and that of his descendants. It lies hidden
under freshly mown English grass.

When he dreamt, it was she who spoke to him
in another language, from another land.
She asked to be remembered as his origin story
every time he saw jacarandas ablaze.

Charm for a Swarm of Bees (A Mistranslation)

"Wio ymbe nim eorphan, oferweorp mid pinre swipram"

When the bees begin to sing, sculpt some earth
with your right hand, stick it under your right right foot, and say:

Here where I understand I will stake my claim.
Listen to the gland speak, lord of us all:
Mightier than Alice, mightier than Mike,
The master of every man's mother. Tongued.

When the bees begin to swim, eat some sand, use your palm,
Scatter it over then, like a soft clout, and say say:

Stay caput on this spot, proud sisters with arms!
Never turn wild wild and take woods.
What is good for you is God for me,
as all men are   nude and tanned.

Meditations of an Immigrant (Cinquaines)

Upstairs
a bus to Deal
I'll beat the hell out of
you heard the Kentish lad. Scratched panes
fog up

*

Angler
on a bulked pier.
He wears waterproof shorts.
Out with the bloody immigrants,
the lot

*

There was
a well so deep
where all the coins were thrown
a stone block where they gathered, cut
some throats

*

Sleep tight
for night is all
there is: the limbs of men
their pain and grief. I too succumb
to this

*

On Earth
not much to see:
a road, few pilgrims, wars . . .
Books rare, but then people could read
the stars

Pyramids in Sand

Among the giant American elms of Central Park,
the Steinway Tower   half finished,   its godly cranes,   its blue sky
glass applied one by one by latinos,   a flimsy lift going up,
down,   we walked under it
on 57th along Billionaires' Row,
where tired horses wreathed in plastic flowers stood in line
and a Bolivian watermelon woman seller
cursed in Aymara at the vagabond
shouting the world's end
was coming
and you better prepare.

*

At the Western Union counter on 78th and 3rd Avenue,
a Colombian cleaning lady sends 100 dollars to her daughter,
she speaks Spanish with the assistant,
who learned the language at home   somewhere in East Harlem
but hardly speaks it now,   they eye each other's gestures,
check they way they roll the r's l's,   how the assistant asks: *firme aquí, no?*
a smirk behind the dirty glass,   the uneasiness as they talk
about the city's foul weather, the new deluxe latino shop selling *arepas,*
they say goodbye in broken English   until next week's pay cheque.

*

The waiter at Amaranth on 62nd
immediately recognises your accent,
brings the menu, asks in Spanish
with a soft Ecuadorian accent
if you're here visiting, or like him
por la economía   for the money.

Elephant & Castle

It wasn't the *Infanta de Castilla*
nor Castile's long-gone elephant
but a shopping centre arcade
where *latinos* dined at La Bodeguita.

Everyone congregates
in the main yellow concourse
at the small *al paso* cafeterías,
they've been talking

of how the leftist mayor
approved the final plans
by Delancey developers
to demolish the run down centre.

A pesar de prometer lo contrario!
el hijo'puta! el descara'o!
And all for a few quid . . .
el cabrón lo pagará bien caro!

They'll tear down the salmon-
pink pachyderm carrying the white
castle turret, as he rises regal
on top of such expensive land.

The grandiose bronze mastodon
especially made for the big market
in 1965, taken from an old pub,
now bulldozed. But he stands

so majestic on a tall pedestal
atop Los Colorados, Tienda Latina
and the *arepa* and *tamales* shop,
as he surveys his dwindling empire.

Crows

Bird of ill omen, I saw you first when I arrived in England back in 1997. You were standing on a wooden bench by Pimlico Tube. After a series of short caws, you flew three times round the hostel I was staying at. I picked up the phone to tell father I wasn't coming back.

Cycles

'We love the things we love for what they are'
— ROBERT FROST

Blackbird's gone
    —until next year's
            bonanza. He left
a simple cup nest full
of dried twigs, hairs
    —courtyard detritus
            barely hanging on
a wisteria climber
that never flowers
        its badly grafted roots
compressed, down
into our house's under
    —side.
It grew faster, taller
        than we first thought.
Love witness, even these
thunderous wrens
    —*Troglodytes* like to catch
hidden flies, tiny-spiders
dangling over light-green
    —leaves, shoots. These signs
            we've learned to read
every English summer
    —almost by chance.

Robin

Your red breast shining
as I dig with my hands
soil on soil. Dusty sun.

Pulling a thorn
when it wasn't needed,
holly blood on my thumb.

I broke your bright-blue eggs
something valuable of mine
now equally beyond repair.

Tilted

Imagine a day in February, lets say the 24th
   lets suppose it is two in the afternoon, and you notice

it is the first sunny day in weeks
    that there is a sudden change

in the air
    a tilt,   a shift

a lick warming your face,
   as sun comes out through a clouded sky.

Imagine a wooden floor room
  filled with sunlight

three opened sash-windows
  facing a leafless maple tree,

where a bird feeder hangs.

Then your mind travels fast, your room
    is not your room anymore,

it is a place you've been to long ago,
      that you can't quite recall.

Imagine *that* room full of birds
    coming to feed,

landing at your hand.

Then, you remember.

Sea-Horse

'There were 180–200 "death flights" in 1977 and 1978, killing thousands of people. When the major gave the order, we just had to drop them. I was not conscious that the order was immoral' – EVIDENCE GIVEN AT COURT BY THE ARGENTINE EX-NAVAL OFFICER ADOLFO SCILINGO, ACCUSED OF CRIMES AGAINST HUMANITY DURING THE SO CALLED 'DIRTY WAR' IN ARGENTINA.

Down there

      sea was a sea you didn't recognise

blindfolded, a whisper—

           don't forget who you are

        on your way

down

   lack of oxygen,

      cells burst open,

         blood-flow to lungs

stops

there is still time   to live   a gasp   a breath of nothing

Sea-horse, *caballito de mar*   will ride on your side

      your tangled language parts reversing roles

   let them know you hover

        in stormy waters of the South Atlantic,   a blue whale

a lost trawler ship

        they were pushed down,

                they were pushed down

      Officer Scilingo danced in a trance

                  on those maddening flights

changing colour,

        clicking heels

Sea-Horse saw it.

Alchemist's Furnace

'Sometimes they put me on to the torture table and stretched me out, tying my hands and feet to a machine which I can't describe since I never saw it, but which gave me the feeling that they were going to tear part of my body off' –Testimony of Dr Norberto Liwsky (file No. 7397). Nunca Más (Never Again), Report of Conadep, 1984

They pulled a hay wagon, cursed the world all the way
to their heavenly downfall. On horseback, crawling,
limping on one foot. Let them taste grass at all costs.

Popes, priests, *dictadores* follow a mad procession.
Hay to enrich them, to fall in love, climbing higher
to see demons above. Five Senses, Seven Sins.

Four elements for a world governed by fodder power.
A slow dance begins to unravel. Time for wild beasts.
Then, a carefully choreographed summit of half-animals.

In a desperate burning tower, naked men on stumps,
bodies decomposing. This a party of the disappeared.
Gone their hay wagon. And they fell down like toads.

The Weight of the Planet: *Variations on Eielson* *

*On the left, my translations of Jorge Eduardo Eielson's poems selected from 'Vivir es una Obra Maestra' (2003), and on the right my variations.

Variations in front of a door	The House of a Thousand Corridors

the door isn't closed
the door isn't closed or open
the door isn't open
the door is never closed
the door is never open or closed
the door is never open
the door has been closed for ever
the door is closed
the door has been open for ever
the door is open

*

Everybody asks me
how I can live a solitary life
on this sky-blue mountain

Nobody can see I am simply
sitting on this chair
staring at an ordinary wall.

*

XXXIX

We didn't have a car
Television or even an umbrella
And when it rained
It simply rained.

I closed the door,
touched the floor.
You said: 'I'm here.' We speak
to forget. The door is a door
of a house that we've been to.
It's now. And from there to the sea.
I said: 'Stay. I prepared maté.'
You open your eyes,
but we leave
anyway.

*

Everybody asks me
how I can live a solitary life
on this violet mountain

Nobody can see I am simply
sitting on this chair
staring at an ordinary wall.

*

XXXIX

I was born *el día
de los muertos*, my sister
cried relentlessly for years.

XXVI

The same musician
Discovered your secret in a corner
    of the closet
Under a pile of dirty clothes
Lay the damned egg
of your apparitions and disappearances.

*

There will be a machine so pure
a perfect copy of itself
with a thousand green eyes
and a thousand scarlet lips
it will be useless
but will have your name
Oh Eternity.

XXVI

The first night I had sex with a man
he told me to wait outside
but I left,
apparently
never to return.

*

When I returned from Argentina
you built a writing studio for me
at the back of our house
and told me
write a poem
for us.

*

Body of earth

All I see on Earth
convinces me I will never be a man
or a woman or an ant
not even an educated person
I don't cut my hair or shave my beard
except when the sky asks me to
The crocodile is my beloved brother
cockroaches my only family
I share with the grass and the toad
the love of rain and with the spider
the art of building castles with saliva
Like this I move forward I move forward still
generally on four legs
two shoes
or beneath a hat

*

Birdwatching

All I could see on Earth
birds – but instead, the sky
lit up; a sunken ship
lost on its way
to the wind farms
I concealed sand
or a hand on my tie,
beside a pig-snail playing golf
I came back, opened
the pores, you were drowning
as if I wasn't there.
What's lost is the hour
spoken by heart.
The house
ate us alive.

An Ideal Day

Morning
Question:
What good shall I do
this day?

5	Rise, affirm, grunt, contrive,
6	eat a fig
7	
8	Swim
9	
10	Murmur
11	(rest, do your accounts, dine, mumble,
12	point out)
13	
14	Work if
15	
16	Promise (shhh)
17	(Put things in their places, supper,
18	music, avoid more diversion)
19	Converse, lie, lick
20	
21	Sleep. Do not disclose,
22	dream. *El sueño que devora*
23	
24	

Noon

Evening
Question: What good
have I done this day?

Night

A Water Poem

Tide times ten *too far,*
uncovered morning,
ridge,
pier & back, water marks on skin,
marked & body stretched
barely salt, barely skin
passed a point. Again
to deep, inside
a song for charms
its bone for bone,
baptised. Tide goes up, it's you
who sleep
on my neck, salty drops

an empty land
a shingle slope,   a
forbidden stretch from here   to
skin
cold on cold,
turned stone
& back to sea, back
to count *uno, dos, tres* a song
& you it's swim it's hour
a watered eye & you,
back home
Te duermes. It's morning sex, water
to cure & tide, its tide

At the Shore

Day breaks the whole, empty
   beach bursting, light
      on the spot where the English sea
        meets a foreign eye.

Globed glassy head of onyx,
   the grey seal surfaces
      in attempt to catch
        distracted chicks adrift.

There are dried carcasses too.
   Bleached hulks at the ashen shore
      of crabs, sharks, ossuaries of green
        bottles exhumed by the sun.

This morning fishermen
   flail their futile tents
      of nylon, neoprene,
        baits drunk in kerosene.

Bald concrete pier on greening stilts,
   its polyester flags of Europe
      replaced one by one
        by the Empire's Magog.

Further out the tankers, cargo ships,
   and prowling border patrols
      telescopes on high alert
        for *desperados* in rubber dinghies.

A trawler fights the tides and birds
    begging behind. Tired trollers
        cast the net and wait
            to gather the odd fish.

I survey the waves atop a mound
    of brown pebbles brought by giant
        shovel cranes that return
            to Dover harbour and the docks.

An immigration team in a large van
    parked on the empty esplanade.
        X-ray machines patrol
            pixels of glowing heat.

Birds Leaving Earth (I)

You can always escape   leave
through a back door   a crack
yellow bird   black augur
los pájaros no van a ninguna parte
there is a fire   somewhere
a recurrent theme   an errant
flock of southern invaders   the
towers burn the sky   a call
explodes in ruby reds   oranges
la selva se enciende   there is no
escape   you can always
lie   about your beginnings
the odd colour   of your exodus
yellow bird   black augur
I stole this   they took that
as you turn   look back
beware   of salt statues
of feathered things   going
in circles   sensing
          the impending night

Birds Leaving Earth (II)

We saw its colours darken
fast beyond the little burning
sky, as we fell for it, the
technicolor migrants, the
exodus to wherever
that end place would've been.
There was no final end
to that sudden flight, no re-
collection of sound
blasts escaping fast,
but a simple trajectory
from A to B, no back
               to that inhospitable
    cobalt globe, that
                   orb going
     a tad mad,
       its nomad
     dwellers
       thrown out.
         Sun turned
      its back to us,
            as all things
       were leaving.

Seraphim

I was transformed and can now return with a pair of wings,
my head turned bright red, my black and yellow dyed wings.

They said I was nearly extinct, that I was kept, bred in captivity,
that they used me for their hats, that they went after my wings.

I am flying now, high above the country, over the River Plate
and Buenos Aires, its low tin-roofed houses, on my wings.

I see the vast Pampas and beyond, the fishermen, the gauchos
at their bonfires, I feel the acrid smoke rising under my wings.

And I see the grave of my father, a place I've never been,
I, Leonardo, on my black and yellow wings.

Immigrant's Boat

The ship that brought me
    had lost its course
        and instead of stopping
            at every sunny harbour,
                greeted by a joyful lighthouse,
                    kept on going from one continent
                    to the next.
A promising Southern Northern sky,
    towards the immensity
        of the open seas, we passed
            many coasts, archipelagos.
                Passengers gathered to look,
                    gossiping in many dialects;
                    Catalan, Sicilian, Basque.

Yet every time
    the courtesy flag was raised
        to dock and land
            at last to disembark,
                oh, again *adieu!*
                    engines' roar, full speed astern,
                    foam surged behind.
The ship's Janus figurehead
    that rocked back and forth,
        would try to drop anchor,
            its periscope filtering
                such luminous *terra firma,*
                    yet kept going, a somnambulist
                  with no walls to bash into.

Despairing, the second,
    third-class passengers,
       their high hopes dashed,
         asked in low tones
           among themselves,
             why their bad luck kept
               following them from home.
At high sea,
    the sound of crashing,
      sea mammals trailing,
        a lone whale closing in
          as blue icebergs surfaced,
            no idle sunbathers
              on the muted deck.
I, frozen in time,
    watched hungry seagulls
      flying low, saw
        tempests quickly form,
          the distant warships ready
            for yet another war,
              as porpoises looked on.
How far yet to go? The ship
    continued, a floating carcass
      adrift, aimless,
        fleeing famine, onslaughts,
          outbreaks. The miseries
            that were the siren call
              to the early twentieth century exodus.

The immigrants of the ship
        that brought me
            never get off, we drift together.
                There among them,
                    my great aunt Gracia, the one
                        with a knotted index,
                            incessantly knitting my socks.
She was the one born aboard,
        baptised by the head cook
            by the grace of God,
                witnessed by captain Raúl,
                    my paternal grandfather,
                        he who got to see almost all
                            the big cities: Liverpool, New York,
                                St. Petersburg, Río Gallegos.
He took the ship's wheel
        but didn't know the course.
            Also on board, my great-
                grandparents: Ramón,
                    his sick wife María,
                        the cursed Sicilian peasants
                            from San Mauro di Castelverde.
Their nine children around,
        dressed in patched black,
            the elders telling *Cosa Nostra* jokes,
                how they had to live
                    with only a little soup,
                        barely a thing to sow
                            on thin war-torn soil.

There was also Atilano,
        Abuelo's short-lived father,
            his thin moustache, his tattered
                Spanish red guitar
                    made at famed Zamora,
                        his felt hat, some bread,
                            his pile of worn-out bags.
Onboard distant cousins, great
        uncles, drifters, blood
            of my own blood,
                a line as thinly stretched
                    as the flimsy boat
                        somehow kept afloat,
                            but erring, unmoored.

Notes

'**Peregrination**': 'Me olvidé de vivir' is a 1977 song by Johnny Hallyday popularised in Spanish by singer and songwriter Julio Iglesias.

'**SS *General Pueyrrédon***': This poem is partially based on the story of my grandfather, a captain of the Argentine merchant Navy who came to England in the 1950s to bring back a large ship being built in the Cammell Laird shipyards at Birkenhead, Liverpool.

'**Island**': A found poem from *Gargantua and Pantagruel* by François Rabelais, translated into English by Thomas Urquhart.

'**Godwanaland**': Refers to the more southerly of two supercontinents (the other being Laurasia), which were once part of the Pangaea supercontinent that existed from approximately 510 to 180 million years ago. This poem was inspired by the work of some of the Concrete Poets of Latin America, among them Oliverio Girondo, Haroldo and Augusto de Campos, and Cecilia Vicuña.

'**Duchamp writes from Argentina**': A reworked found poem from a letter the French artist wrote to Ettie Stettheimer in November 1918, after a nine-month visit to Buenos Aires.

'**Victoria Ocampo Writes About Meeting Virginia Woolf**': A reworked found poem after one of the letters written by Argentine writer and intellectual Victoria Ocampo to Virginia Woolf in 1934, shortly after they met in London.

'Charm for a Journey (A Mistranslation)' and 'Charm for a Swarm of Bees (A Mistranslation)': These poems are based on the twelve Anglo-Saxon metrical charms written in Old English.

'Folklore Tale': According to the Guaraní legend of the jacaranda, a sacred tree native to the Amazon, a bird deposited a priestess known as Daughter of the Moon on top of the tree. The priestess descended and lived among the villagers, with whom she shared her knowledge of the universe.

'Elephant & Castle': The shopping centre in Elephant & Castle was a traditionally important site for the Latin American community in London. In spite of a lengthy local campaign and numerous protests it was demolished by property developers Delancey, who will turn the site into a new 'town centre'.

'Alchemist's Furnace': A poem inspired by 'The Haywain Triptych' (1516) by Hieronymus Bosch and the events of the military dictatorship that ruled Argentina from 1976 to 1983.

'Seraphim': This is a poem after 'Ghazal: Wings', by 14-year-old Afghani student Halema Malak, included in the anthology 'England Poems from a School' (Picador, 2018). I was inspired by and borrow several lines of her poem, particularly the final line, 'I, Halema, on my black wings', to explore themes of migration, heritage and diaspora in my own experiences as a Latinx migrant.

Acknowledgements

Thanks are due to the editors of the following publications in which some of these poems, or versions of them, have previously appeared:

And Other Poems, *harana poetry*, *The Literary Consultancy*, *Modern Poetry in Translation*, *The Morning Star*, *National Poetry Library (Southbank Centre)*, *PN Review*, *POETRY*, *The Poetry Review*, *Ten Poets of the New Generation* (Bloodaxe), *Un Nuevo Sol/British Latinx Writers* (flipped eye), *The White Review*, *Why Poetry?–The Lunar Poetry Podcasts Anthology* (Verve).

'At the Shore', 'Birds Leaving Earth I', 'Birds Leaving Earth II', 'Pyramids in Sand', and 'Immigrant's Boat' were commissioned by the National Poetry Library to mark the centennial of Lawrence Ferlinghetti. They were also part of the exhibition at the Southbank Centre 'A 21st Century Ferlinghetti', which coincided with the 50th anniversary of *Poetry International*, a biennial festival celebrating poetry from all over the world.

First and foremost I would like to thank Nathalie Teitler, who, as well as being a dear friend and an unflinching mentor, took uncounted hours to read, re-read and advise on all aspects of this book. It is down to her initial faith that I began to take my writing seriously in English. Her encouragement is ongoing and necessary. I would also like to thank the whole Complete Works Family for their support and friendship, and to the Latinx familia in the UK and elsewhere for giving me a sense of community. A special thank you to my editor Parisa Ebrahimi for her invaluable advice, vision and generosity, as well as to the entire team at Chatto &

Windus. Parisa's meticulous engagement has taken my poetry to a level that was entirely new to me. My gratitude also to the colleagues and mentors for reading and advising on the manuscript. Their names are not listed but they know who they are. Thank you also to Chris McCabe, the National Poetry Librarian, for commissioning some of the poems in this book. With gratitude to the Society of Authors for their generous grant, which allowed me to finish this book during the lockdown period. As ever, the support of loved ones means that my work falls on kindly ears, which is why my family in Argentina and my extended family in the UK continue to give me warm encouragement. Without that, this book would not have been possible.

Gracias a todos!